SCHOLASTIC

TRUE OR FALSE

Dangerous Animals

D1041490

BY MELVIN AND GILDA BERGER

Front cover: DLILLC/Corbis; Page 3: Steve Bloom Images/Alamy; Page 4: Florida Images/
Alamy; Page 5: Steve Bloom Images/Alamy; Page 6: Uwe Skrzypczak/Alamy; Page 7 &
back cover: DLILLC/Corbis; Page 8: Chris Fredriksson/Alamy; Page 9: Darren Bennett/
Animals Animals; Page 10: Images&Stories/Alamy; Page 11: Kitch Bain/Shutterstock;
Page 12: Fritz Polking/Peter Arnold Inc.; Page 13: EcoPrint/Shutterstock; Page 14: Ann and
Steve Toon/Alamy; Page 15: Brandon Cole Marine Photography/Alamy; Page 16: Images
of Africa Photobank/Alamy; Page 17 & back cover: Mary Ann McDonald/Corbis; Page 18:
C. W. Schwartz/Animals Animals; Page 19: J&B Photographers/Animals Animals; Page 20:
Images of Africa Photobank/Alamy; Page 21: Michael DeFreitas Central America/Alamy;
Page 22 & back cover: Brent Ward/Alamy; Page 23: wildworld/Alamy; Page 24: Wolfgang
Kaehler/Alamy; Page 25: Rusty Dodson/Shutterstock; Page 26: Kennan Ward/Corbis; Page
27: Stephen Frink Collection/Alamy; Page 28: Firefly Productions/Corbis; Page 29: David
Aubrey/Photo Researchers, Inc.; Page 30: Morales/age fotostock; Page 31: Gary Bell/Getty
Images, Inc.; Page 32: Paul Sutherland/Getty Images, Inc.; Page 33: Paul Ives/Alamy; Page 34:
Anthony Marsh/Alamy; Page 35: David Hall/Getty Images, Inc.; Page 36: Jeffrey L. Rotman/
Corbis; Page 37: David Fleetham/Alamy; Page 38: Jeffrey L. Rotman/Corbis; Page 39: Jim
West/Alamy; Page 40: Darren Bennett/Animals Animals; Page 41: WildPictures/Alamy;
Page 42: Patrick Lynch/Alamy; Page 43: Frans Lanting/Corbis; Page 44: ARCO/D. Usher/age
fotostock; Page 45: Johner Images/Alamy; Page 46: MedicalRF.com/Corbis.

Text copyright © 2009 by Melvin and Gilda Berger
All rights reserved. Published by Scholastic Inc., *Publishers since 1920.*
SCHOLASTIC and associated logos are trademarks and /or
registered trademarks of Scholastic Inc.

No part of this publication may be reproduced, stored in a retrieval system, or
transmitted in any form or by any means, electronic, mechanical, photocopying,
recording, or otherwise, without written permission of the publisher. For information
regarding permission, write to Scholastic Inc., Attention: Permissions Department,
557 Broadway, New York, NY 10012.

ISBN-13: 978-0-545-00395-7
ISBN-10: 0-545-00395-4

10 9   12 13

Printed in the U.S.A.   40
First printing, January 2009
Book design by Nancy Sabato

Big animals are more dangerous than small ones.

TRUE OR FALSE?

FALSE! Dangerous animals can be big or small.

Some dangerous animals are big and powerful. They kill with their sharp teeth or mighty paws. But many other dangerous animals are small and weak. They kill with poison or with harmful viruses and bacteria. Some dangerous animals attack and kill prey for food. Others kill to protect themselves or their young from enemies.

The tiny black widow spider is the deadliest spider in North America.

4

Male lions do most of the hunting.

TRUE OR FALSE?

FALSE! Female lions usually hunt and kill the prey.

A female lion, or lioness, chases prey for food. The rest of the pride watches and waits. When the lioness gets close to the prey, she pulls it down. Then she clamps her teeth around its neck or nose. The animal stops breathing. Then the other lions and lionesses come in for the meal.

Lions eat first, then lionesses, and finally lion cubs.

Tigers have the sharpest teeth of all big cats.

TRUE OR FALSE?

TRUE! Tigers' back teeth are as sharp as knives.

A tiger's teeth can cut through flesh like a hot knife through butter. After a tiger has caught and killed its prey, the big cat hides the body. Tigers sometimes drag their prey to the side of a river or lake. This lets the tigers drink while they eat. After they eat, they cover the remains with leaves to protect it from scavengers. Tigers that attack humans are usually old, with weak teeth.

A tiger can take three or four days to eat a large buffalo or wild pig.

Grizzly bears often harm humans.

TRUE OR FALSE?

FALSE! Grizzly bears hunt fish, deer, and squirrels—not people.

Grizzly bears are huge, fast, and very dangerous. They use their sharp teeth and claws to catch food. But grizzly bears generally avoid people. Only rarely will a very hungry or frightened grizzly charge someone. Then the bear can break the person's neck or back with a swift blow from its powerful front paws.

The grizzly bear is one of the biggest and strongest land animals in North America.

Male hippopotamuses often fight. TRUE OR FALSE?

TRUE! Male hippos battle other males for control of a territory.

Hippos have huge teeth. They use them to dig up and chew plants, which are their main food. But they also use their teeth as weapons. One angry hippo rushes toward another with mouth wide open and teeth showing. Demonstrating their great strength, the beasts swing their heads like sledgehammers and bite each other.

A struggle between two male hippos often ends in death for one or both.

Hyenas
are noisy
hunters.

TRUE
OR
FALSE?

TRUE!

When catching prey, hyenas often make noises that sound like crazy laughter.

Hyenas are smart, cunning hunters and scavengers. Alone, they usually catch small prey such as lizards, snakes, and birds. But working together, large groups, or clans, of hyenas can bring down zebras, gazelles, antelopes, buffalo, and rhinoceroses. The hyenas rip the prey apart and quickly eat the whole body—horns, hooves, and all.

Hyenas and lions often fight one another over the same prey.

Crocodiles
drown their
prey.

TRUE
OR
FALSE?

TRUE! A crocodile holds its prey underwater until it stops breathing.

A crocodile usually lies and waits in the water to spot its prey. Then it slowly glides toward the victim. When it gets close, the crocodile uses its powerful jaws to grab the animal. With a lot of splashing, the crocodile drags the prey underwater, drowns it, and tears off chunks or swallows it whole. Many different animals, from fish to zebras, can be dinner for a crocodile.

Crocodiles eat their prey in the water.

The
rattlesnake
is one of
the most
dangerous
snakes.

TRUE
OR
FALSE?

TRUE! Rattlesnakes use venom, or poison, to kill prey.

The rattlesnake injects its poison through long, hollow teeth, called fangs. The fangs are on the roof of the snake's mouth. They are folded back until the rattler strikes. Then the fangs snap down. They point down as the snake lunges forward to deliver the poison. A rattlesnake's poison is so powerful that it can kill large animals and even people.

The larger the snake, the more poison it can deliver in one bite.

Cape buffalo
kill with their
horns. TRUE
OR
FALSE?

TRUE! Cape buffalo attack their enemies headfirst.

The Cape buffalo is one of the most dangerous creatures in Africa. Anything that comes close, from a lion to a person, can expect a knock-down, drag-out fight. The Cape buffalo charges its attacker at full speed. Using its horns, the Cape buffalo stabs again and again. More hunters in Africa may be killed by Cape buffalo than by any other animal.

The Cape buffalo kills animals, but it only eats plants.

The beautiful poison dart frog is not really poisonous.

TRUE OR FALSE?

FALSE!

The poison from just one frog is enough to kill one hundred people. The poison dart frog's poison oozes out through tiny holes in its skin. Any attacker that tries to eat the frog—or even just touch it—will die or be paralyzed. Hunters in Central and South America sometimes rub the poison onto their darts and arrows. Animals hit with a poisoned dart or arrow die soon after.

The frogs with the brightest colors often have the strongest poison.

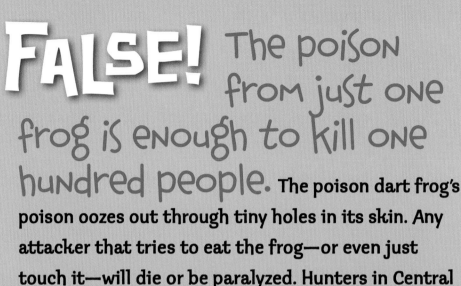

The Komodo dragon mainly uses its eyes to find prey.

TRUE or FALSE?

FALSE! The Komodo dragon usually sniffs out prey with its huge forked tongue.

The dragon's giant tongue picks up the smell of pigs, deer, snakes, or even humans. Then the beast hides and lies in wait for the prey. At the right moment, the lizard charges out and gives chase. It sinks its sharp teeth into the victim. Even if the animal escapes the dragon's jaws, poisonous germs from the lizard's saliva enter the wound. Within twenty-four hours, the prey falls to the ground and dies of blood poisoning.

The Komodo dragon can smell prey from as far as 6 miles (9.7 kilometers) away.

The Gila monster kills with one quick bite.

TRUE OR FALSE?

FALSE!

The Gila monster kills by biting its prey and releasing poison into the wound. The Gila monster tracks prey by flicking its forked tongue. Then the lizard sneaks up and bites the prey before it can get away. Poison flows out through the grooves in the Gila monster's teeth as it holds on to its prey. Then the lizard may chew so that the poison goes deeper into the wound. But most of the time, Gila monsters don't chew their food; they swallow it whole.

The poison can easily kill rodents, frogs lizards, and insects, but rarely humans.

TRUE
OR
FALSE?

The great white
shark eats more
people than any
other fish does.

FALSE! The great white shark sometimes bites people, but it never eats them.

The great white shark can go weeks between meals. But its diet is mostly seals, sea turtles, and large fish. Only rarely does a great white shark bite a person. Each year, there are two to three attacks on humans in the United States. Dogs kill more people in a year than great whites do.

The great white shark has about 3,000 teeth; humans only have 32 teeth.

killer
piranha fish
live in the
ocean.

TRUE
OR
FALSE?

FALSE! Piranhas live in rivers in South America.

Piranhas are one of the most dangerous freshwater fish. Most swim alone and feed on smaller fish. The piranha's razor-sharp teeth quickly kill its victims. Sometimes, though, piranhas swim in groups of a hundred or more. Together, the group may occasionally attack larger animals that wade into the water for a drink.

Piranhas rarely attack people.

A box jellyfish can poison you even after it dies.

TRUE OR FALSE?

TRUE!

A box jellyfish that washes up on a beach stays poisonous for a while. A living box jellyfish looks like an upside-down box floating in the ocean. Sixty very long, thin strings, called tentacles, hang down from the "box." When other sea creatures swim by and touch the box jellyfish, chemicals from their bodies trigger stinging cells on the tentacles. They shoot out many bits of poisonous thread. In a flash, the poison paralyzes and kills the creature.

Some species of box jellyfish can cause heart failure and death within minutes.

Lionfish sting but don't bite.

TRUE OR FALSE?

TRUE! Lionfish sting with their sharp, poisonous spines.

When in danger, a lionfish raises the needlelike spines on its back. Each spine is filled with poison. The lionfish swims toward its attacker with its spines pointing forward, ready to sting. The poison is strong enough to kill most prey. A person unlucky enough to be stung by a lionfish gets a painful wound but does not die.

Lionfish only use their poison to protect themselves, not to catch prey.

A puffer
fish is deadly
if eaten by
a human.

TRUE
OR
FALSE?

TRUE! Eating a puffer fish can kill you.

Many people, especially in Japan, love the taste of puffer fish. But some puffer fish organs contain a very powerful poison. There are chefs in Japan who know how to remove all the poison sacs. Yet every year a few people eat the fish and die. Puffer fish are named for the way they puff themselves up with water to avoid capture.

Enemies are rarely able to bite or swallow a puffed-up puffer fish.

A blue-ringed octopus has poisonous arms.

TRUE or FALSE?

FALSE! The arms of the blue-ringed octopus are lined with harmless suckers.

The dangerous part of the blue-ringed octopus is its poisonous saliva. A single bite injects a deadly poison into the victim. Even though the blue-ringed octopus is only the size of a golf ball, its poison is very powerful. Often it kills in minutes. Many people die from the bite of a pretty blue-ringed octopus when they step on the animal or pick it up for a closer look.

The poison of the blue-ringed octopus is probably stronger tha that of any land anima

Eagles kill with their sharp beaks.

TRUE OR FALSE?

TRUE! Eagles catch and kill prey with their claws, and use their beaks to bite the prey and kill it.

Eagles fly over water looking for fish swimming near the surface. They also soar high over land searching the ground for rabbits or mice. When they spot their prey, the eagles swoop down to grab it with their long, sharp claws, or talons. No bird, mouse, or rabbit can escape the deep clutch of an eagle's spearlike talons.

Eagles can spot their prey from as high as 2 miles (3.2 kilometers) in the air.

A tiny fire ant
can bring down
a large animal
or human with
its sting.

TRUE
OR
FALSE?

FALSE! A fire ant cannot kill a large creature by itself.

Fire ants are most dangerous when they sting in great numbers and at the same time. Each ant stings again and again, turning itself around in a circle. The ants keep up this stinging frenzy for a long time. People stung by fire ants say it feels like burning matches held against their skin. Allergic reactions to fire ant stings may be life-threatening.

Fire ants can be found in the Southeastern United States.

Scorpions bite their prey.

TRUE OR FALSE?

FALSE! Scorpions have mouths but do not bite.

Instead of biting, scorpions sting their victims. They whip up the sharp, curved stinger at the end of their tails. *ZAP!* They send a shot of poison into an insect or small animal. The scorpion then grabs its prey and breaks it into tiny pieces. Then the scorpion squirts digestive juices on the pieces, which turn to liquid. *SLURP!* The scorpion sucks up its tasty meal.

A scorpion that is ready to attack opens it claws and raises its tail.

The mosquito is the most dangerous animal in the world.

TRUE OR FALSE?

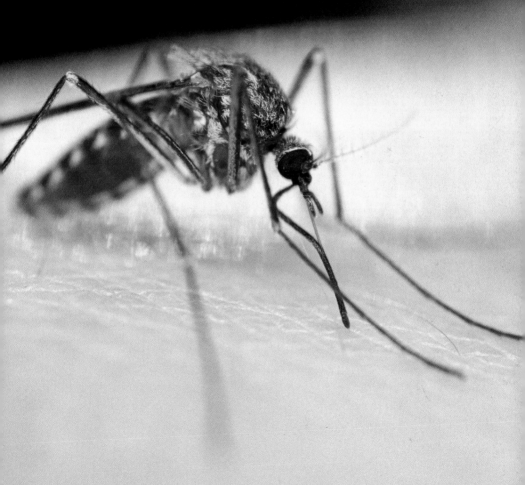

TRUE!

worldwide, mosquitoes kill more people than any other dangerous animal does. When a mosquito lands on a person's skin, it instantly draws a tiny drop of blood. Sometimes the blood contains germs. The mosquito carries the germs to the next creature it bites. The germs spread and make many people sick. Malaria and yellow fever are some of the deadly human diseases transmitted by mosquitoes.

Mosquitoes cause more than one million deaths a year worldwide.

Index

B

bacteria, harmful, 4

beaks, of eagles, 39—40

buffalo, Cape

  diet of, 20

  horns of, 19—20

C

claws, of grizzly bears, 10

crocodiles

  diet of, 16

  drowning prey, 15—16

D

dangerous animals, big or small, 3—4

diseases, mosquito-transmitted, 46

E

eagles

  killing prey, 39—40

  sharp beaks of, 39—40

  talons of, 40

  vision of, 40

F

fighting

  by Cape buffalo, 20

  between male hippopotamuses, 11—12

fire ants, sting of, 41—42

fish

  great white sharks, 27—28

  lionfish, 33—34

  piranhas, 29—30

  puffer fish, 35—36

frogs, poison dart, 21—22

G

Gila monsters, killing prey, 25—26

grizzly bears, harming humans, 9—10

H

hippopotamuses, males fighting, 11—12

horns, of Cape buffalo, 19—20

humans

  fire ant attacks on, 42

  great white shark attacks on, 28

  grizzly bear attacks on, 10

  hunting with poison darts, 22

  mosquito-transmitted diseases of, 46

  piranha fish attacks on, 30

hunting

  by lions, 5—6

  by hyena clans, 14

  with poison darts, 22

hyenas, "laughing," 13—14

I

insects

  fire ants, 41—42

  mosquitoes, 45—46

J

jellyfish, box, poison of, 31—32

K

Komodo dragons, finding prey, 23—24

L

lionfish, sting of, 33—34